Voices from Vilna

Helen & Jack

Lots of love to wonderful
Friends

Love Hilane & Jack

Voices from Vilna

Helaine Shoag Greenberg

*Yiddish translated by Sylvia Schildt
and Rita Ratson*
Polish translated by Maria Pietka

iUniverse, Inc.
New York Lincoln Shanghai

Voices from Vilna

iUniverse books may be ordered through booksellers or by contacting:

iUniverse
2021 Pine Lake Road, Suite 100
Lincoln, NE 68512
www.iuniverse.com
1-800-Authors (1-800-288-4677)

ISBN-13: 978-0-595-39737-2 (pbk)
ISBN-13: 978-0-595-84143-1 (ebk)
ISBN-10: 0-595-39737-9 (pbk)
ISBN-10: 0-595-84143-0 (ebk)

Printed in the United States of America

"Sometimes a forest burns down, but once in a while you find a seedling." An old man from Vilna made this remark when we recently met.

Contents

Photographs

Acknowledgements

I thank the Jewish Gen ShtetlSchleppers Project in Houston, Texas for enabling me to visit the sites where these letters took place. I owe a special thanks to Galina Baranova, archivist at the Lithuanian National Museum, and to our guide extraordinaire Regina Kopilevich who gave us a past by handing us a family tree. Now I too, along with my Yankee friends, can be related to the ages. The birth and death records suggest that the legend about the family name Shoag is true. I also thank Rachel Kastanian at the Vilna Gaon Jewish State Museum of Lithuania for suggesting this project.

The author thanks Nancy Nicholas for her editorial assistance.

Introduction of
the Letter Writers

After my parents died in 1984, in the basement of their house in Jeannette, Pennsylvania, I found a treasure of family letters sent between 1929 and 1940 from what is now Vilnius, Lithuania. After World War I, the period of the early letters, the city became Wilno, Poland, until it was returned to Lithuania immediately before the Second World War. To the Jewish citizens of this illustrious and beloved city, however, it was always the Yiddish Vilna, the "Jerusalem of the North," home of the learned and famous rabbi, Vilna Gaon.

The early letters (1929–1934) were from Wolf Shoag in Vilna to his love Ida Levin (Chayela in the letters) in the United States. When Frank and Mary Levin, Ida's parents, brought their daughter back to Vilna in 1929 to visit relatives, Ida and Wolf met and fell in love. Wolf learned English to write to Ida. Wolf and Ida, my parents, got married in the United States in 1934. The next letters, dated 1938, were sent to the American Consul General in Warsaw, Poland from a United States congressman as part of an effort to help Wolf get some of his family out of Europe. The final letters, translated from Yiddish, are from Moses Mattathias Shoag, Wolf's father and my grandfather, and from Wolf's sister, my aunt, Roza Shoag Koslovska.

I feel privileged to have been able to become intimate with these relatives through their letters. I decided to write my family's story after a visit I made to Vilna in May 2000 to present one important letter to Rachel Kastanian, the Director of the Vilna Gaon Jewish Museum. The museum did not have primary documents from the

1930s, and she urged me to write about the ones I had found. The letters describe the prelude to the horrors of World War II and the Holocaust from a personal perspective. Moses and Roza seemed to know what would happen, but they kept some hope alive. I wrote this so their voices might be heard.

A brief family history: Moses Mattathias Shoag, his wife, Fagel Rochel, and his brother Benjamin and his family lived in Snipiskes, a suburb of Vilnius, across the Green Bridge. Moses and Fagel Rochel made their living from a store that carried dry goods, bolts of cloth, and shoes, located in the front of their home, at 51/52 Wilkomienska Street. They had six children, three boys and three girls, all born around the turn of the century. In birth order they were Roza, Beyle, Wolf, Shia, Israel and Sonia. Moses was a strict, religious man who went to the synagogue every day, while Fagel took care of the children and the store and did good works in the community.

Fagel and Moses Shoag

My father, Wolf, loved and respected his mother and I suspect may have feared his father. During World War I, Wolf and Roza, the oldest girl, had been sent with the store goods to relatives in Belarus and did not see their parents until the war ended. We know little about his sister Beyle Cutler because Wolf would never talk about his family, except to tell an occasional anecdote or relate a little World War I history. That is one reason why these letters are such a treasure. His youngest sister, Sonia, married Rabbi Cypkiewitz and moved to a town near Traube, Belarus.

Wolf's brother Shia, while attending the Philosophy Faculty of the University of Vilnius in 1932, was pushed from a second floor balcony because he was a Jew. A lifelong Zionist, he married his sweetheart, Lisa Kantorovieins, and fled to Palestine that year. I found the youngest brother Israel, who suffered from tuberculosis, on the JewishGen website which lists those murdered during the war. He was shot in 1941 in Myadel, Belarus, a town near his mother's hometown of Traube. After World War II, the large family's only survivors were Wolf and Shia.

Interspersed with the original letters are thoughts I would have spoken to my father had we visited his Vilna together, as we had once planned. I owed him this trip. Since we never made it together, I have invented letters to him describing my trip and the emotional impact of being "back" where my ancestors had lived for 200 years.

THE EARLY 1930s

Philadelphia, PA April 22, 2000

Dear Dad,

For forty years I have felt guilty about our not going together to Vilna, but I am finally keeping my promise to you and returning. I'm so sorry we could not have gone together. My excuse for not having taken you is that the Russian history professor at Connecticut College disappeared behind the Iron Curtain and I was afraid you, born there, might not have gotten out. While I'm there I'm going to try to find out about your brother and three sisters who perished under the Nazis. You could never talk about them. I'm going to try to find your old house in Vilna. I'm also going to visit Traube, Belarus where Grandma Shoag and Grandma Levin grew up. I'm looking forward to discovering my ancestors even posthumously. I'm hoping to find my own genealogy as my gentile friends have. I want to belong to the ages too.

I found the old family photographs from Lithuania, the love letters to Mom and the letters from your family in Vilna in the late 1930's under the Life magazines, in the little basement room where the canned goods were stored, and I had the Yiddish translated. Those last letters are so full of despair; it is no wonder you could not speak about your family.

I love you, Helaine

Vilna, May 2, 2000

Dear Dad,

Here I am in Vilnius, Lithuania walking the streets that our ances-tors walked 200 years ago. What an awesome experience! The Jewish Genealogy Society based in Houston planned the trip, arranged for hotels and travel and for our wonderful multilingual guide, Regina. She is about thirty-six and was a physics major at the University of Vilnius but is making more money being a guide. There are ten of us staying at a lovely new hotel called Stakliai or Candlestick in the Old Town. Yes, I know this is the site where the Jewish ghetto stood. It is so pretty that it is hard to imagine what terrible events happened here.

We flew here from clean, modern Helsinki to a drab, square, Soviet-style, cement-block airport. During the drive from the air-port we passed unadorned, cement-block apartment houses. When we reached the city proper, I had a real jolt seeing charming Renaissance, Baroque and Classic churches and government build-ings. I was surprised at the sophistication of this Baltic town. I had expected to be traveling back in time to an early part of the twen-tieth century, the time of my grandparents and your childhood, the time of the pictures under the magazines. Those old-fashioned black and white images were of people in front of tiny, wooden houses with tin roofs. Were they taken in the poorer section of town over the Green Bridge? This Stikliai Hotel is part of a French hotel chain with elegant French furniture and matching white and blue scenes on the bedcovers and wallpaper. It is located in the Old Town, now a UNESCO Historic Site, full of restored buildings from the seventeenth and eighteenth centuries and even some rel-

ics from the time of the city's founding, 1323. I can't believe I'm here. I feel defiant: "We Shoags came back to our city."

More tomorrow. My love, joy and longing,
Helaine

P.S. The guide said there are about 100 Jewish families here, and one synagogue remains open. The young rabbi is from Boston.

May 3, 2000

Dear Dad,

Last night I played the family history tape you made in Jeannette. It was good to hear your voice back in your hometown. What you said on the tape about the first Shoag seemed more immediate hearing it here:.

"The time was the late 1700s. Vilna was a blossoming Jewish center. It was around the time of the great and learned Vilna Gaon. A young man named Aryah ("lion" in Hebrew) ben Moses was under the employ of the Polish Earl Sudervianski and managed the Earl's lands in Lithuania. In those years, Lithuania was part of greater Poland. The earl closed out his holdings, and his employees and their families had to move off the land. Aryah took a horse and buggy and moved near Vilna to Wilkomierska Ulca Street. Tsar Alexander I decreed that all citizens must take last names for purposes of tax collection, for his many wars, I suppose. Aryah ben Moses was appointed as a tax collector for the Tsar. As Aryah was a good chazzan (a singer of Hebrew prayers) and had to announce the new law of taking a last name, he chose a synagogue as the place to pronounce the tsar's command. This ancestor had just finished reading a chapter in Amos,

"When the Lion roars, who is not afraid." In Hebrew the words are "Aryah Shoag." He then announced the decree for the taking of last names and stated his last name Shoag, "Roar."

May 4, 2000

Dear Dad,

I'm elated! We went as a group to the Lithuanian National Archives. I had written ahead and sent some money, $80 to be exact. To my great joy, the archivist handed me a family tree that she had put together using several, old leather-bound books. I have found documentation for the only family oral history you would give us by finding Aryah as the first Shoag born in 1780. It is as you said. We can trace the family back to 1780. I am thrilled. All the other names were Moses, Wolf and Aryah repeated every other generation following the Jewish custom of honoring a close relative who had died. You would never speak about your siblings. I guess it was too painful, but I have found their names: two brothers (Israel and Shia) and three sisters (Roza, Sonia and Beyle). Thank you. I love you. H

In 1991, Lithuania and the other Baltic states joined the Western economic market, freeing themselves from Communism. Belarus remained a Communist country.

May 5, 2000 Traube, Belarus

Dear Dad,

Here I am in Belarus, so poor compared to Lithuania. We drove for about an hour and a half on good two-lane roads in Lithuania past flat, green farmland with a few small forests scattered in between. It is May, so I could not tell what crops are planted. We were detained at a nondescript tollbooth at the border for a short time *showing passports and buying $60 worth of Russian rubles each. Unlike Vilna, Belarus still looks just as I expected from our 1929 pictures. It remains poor, the roads narrow and pot-holed. Drab, brown wooden houses with gray tin roofs line the road. A few of them are painted yellow and green. We stopped at several small shops to buy a lunch of radishes and hard salami. Empty white shelves lined the walls. In Lithuania, the stores had been filled with all kinds of Western-style goods.*

You probably remember Oshmena, the largest town in the district. It has one hotel, a Soviet gray box. After registering with the police by presenting a passport and giving information about our plans in Belarus, I took pictures of Lenin's statue outside the local Communist Party Headquarters. I must have attracted the attention of a suspicious policeman because he came over with the Communist Party Chief. The party chief was in his early fifties and spoke softly and kindly to me. I told him we were looking for any Jews who remained in the town. He promptly called the only old lady who had returned, but she was not home. He remarked that we could send money, a few thousand dollars, to build a fence around the overrun Jewish cemetery. "People are poor here and need work," he explained.

The Hotel Oshmena has a large empty lobby except for one desk, a couch and a kiosk for check-in. The small bedrooms on the second floor run along each side of the large, dimly lit hallway. Our rooms were not dirty, just very worn looking., There was a rag rug, maybe beige in its former life, and two iron single beds with worn white sheets. A box radio blasting a woman's voice seemed to glare at my guide and me from the wall. The tiny, shared bathroom has a sink and toilet. Its pipes are painted light blue, but there was no toilet paper or soap. The floor cover is worn gray linoleum. We ate hard meat cubes and peas for dinner in the hotel dining room which was dark and shabby but clean, like the hotel room. The people may be poor, but they really like to dance to loud old-fashioned music, Russian ballads from the fifties, I suspect. The five-piece band tried their best. We joined in, but no one seemed to notice us.

I am so excited to visit Traube, home of both my grandmothers. Traube must be twenty minutes from Oshmena. The town has one

Eastern Orthodox Church. Three shabbily dressed old men offered to show us where the old synagogue had been. They would not take money from Regina, the guide, "Your story is our story. We all have lost much caught between the Bolsheviks and the Nazis." They led us to the spot where the synagogue had been. I could picture my grandmothers and their parents, my great-grandparents, entering a wooden building with a clerestory, like pictures I've seen of the way synagogues were built then, to attend services. To me, it is hallowed ground. There are a few red brick buildings on the main street, and the old men told us that the Jews had businesses there before the war.

I know the story of Grandma Fagel Shoag coming back to Traube to ask her 13-year-old distant cousin Mariasha Levine to come to Vilna to babysit for your older sisters, who were little girls then. I know she finally met Grandpa Levin, they married, and went to America when she was twenty. That was 1902.

Dad, the Jewish cemetery, about one mile down the road, is in ruins, overrun by the forest. The gravestones are knocked down. We turned them over looking for ancestral names to list for the Society records. We found names like Weiner, Kaslovsky, Binakonsky, but no one from our family.

Ten miles from this cemetery, a small monument stands at the entrance to the Evia forest. From the family letters, I suspect that this is where your sister, my Aunt Sonia Shoag Cykiewitz, may have been taken to be shot. I am too sad to talk. During the trip back to Vilnius, the border guards made us wait, but only for one hour.

Should I tell you all this? Is it too much?

H

May 7, 2000

Dear Dad,

Wonder of wonders has happened! When we returned to Vilna, I crossed the Green Bridge into their Snipiskus—your Snipishook, and, Dad, I think I've found your house! Wonderful Regina pulled out an old map and I a new one. We searched through the new buildings and the streets with new names. We found what we thought could be 51-52 Wilkomieska Street, your address on the old letters. Regina was as excited as I was. The lot has two houses placed in an L shape with a courtyard on the side, just as you described. They are stucco now, not wood, but the roof is tin and the address is real, printed on the green letterbox on the wooden gate outside the courtyard. I guess you would be sad here.

I have a picture of handsome you and skinny Mom seated in front of your house when she was eighteen and had returned with her parents for a visit. You were twenty-five. There is a bigger building across the street that might have been the Jewish Hospital that your sister Roza wrote about. This must be it.

Ida Levin and Wolf Shoag

Dad, I brought all the old letters with me. There are about sixty of them. Yours are in English and easy to read. They are all on faded stationery-size white paper. The translator complained about the difficulty in reading sixty-year-old handwritten Yiddish. I wish I had Mom's responses to your letters. You must have left them behind when you came to America in 1934 to marry her.

You told me your Dad had a dry goods and shoe store on this site. It must have been in the front of your house. His brother Benjamin had a grocery store in the front of his house. Their 'liberated' wives worked in the store, and these religious brothers went to pray at their own respective synagogues every day.

I'm sitting on an old wooden bench across from the wooden gate to your house hoping someone will come out. I'm not sure I want to meet them, though. It was sixty years ago.

51-52 Wilkomieska Street

I'm reading these letters you wrote to Mom in the early thirties. I'm so glad Mom's parents came to the USA in 1902. I'm glad they brought Mom here to visit relatives when she was in college in the summer of 1929. I'm so glad you had the foresight to know you had to leave and the luck to fall in love with Mom. What a romance. Four years of communication by letter. From your letters, I see how troubled you were about what was happening and how anxious you were to leave Europe. This is one of the first letters I have in my possession. I had it translated from the Yiddish.

Wilno, Poland September 20, 1929

Dear Ida,

Your short letter made me very happy. It is very difficult to write to you the feelings that I had receiving your letter. It is difficult to travel through a world in a letter and a letter is but discussion. We are now focused on the events in Eretz Israel. The ideal of the Jews in greater Poland is to have large demonstrations in New York and Washington streets in support of founding a Jewish state. This will show strength.

With me, everything is as it was, nothing more, something is missing (a longing for you). If you would be able to answer me on this, I would be very happy, because I cannot give myself an answer. I kiss you "Bubbele" (sweetie).

Give a heartfelt regard to your father, mother, and the whole family and the same also from our neighbors.

Zev (Wolf in Hebrew)

I am taking English lessons and will soon be able to write you in English.

During the nineteenth and early twentieth centuries, Lithuanians, Poles, and Jews lived in relative harmony united against their common enemy, the Russians. Jews were allowed to have their own institutions. At the end of World War I, when the economy was shattered, farmers moved into cities and took over the traditionally Jewish role of small merchants. The Jews went into economic decline. By the early 1930s, Fascism was on the rise in Germany. Eastern Europe was caught between Fascism and Communism. Lithuanians, hating the Russians, followed the German lead. Lithuanian Jews became scapegoats; more than ninety percent were eventually killed.

May 7, later in the day, 2000

Dear Dad,

How fascinating these letters are now that I am here where they were written. I can't stop reading them, and as I read I can see your house. Knowing the history of the period makes the letters most poignant.

Love, H

Wilno, December 2, 1932

Dear Ida,

Yesterday anti-Semitic excesses began at the Vilnius University. Christian students attacked their Jewish colleagues and events befell girl students. (They were raped.) I am enclosing a newspaper, which will make the situation clear to you. The future for the Jews in Poland is a desperate one. Imagine these students are to be our future leaders and we will have to depend on them. You won't find everything so detailed in the paper for they fear confiscation here. Our parents compel us to remain at home in the evenings, but you can imagine with what a heart we do so, knowing that Jews are beaten in the streets and our duty is to defend the Jewish honor. But I pity mother.

Ida, my brother Shia was pushed from a second floor balcony at the University. He has had enough and is leaving for Israel with his sweetheart as soon as possible.

I kiss you,
Wolf

May 7, later in the day, 2000

Goodness Dad, your English is fantastic. Sometimes the phrases are backward but they are all understandable. I guess speaking several languages like Yiddish, Polish, Russian and a little German can help.

What a horrid thing to do. No wonder Uncle Shia left. Now I know why he went to Israel.

Love, H

Wilno, Dec. 13, 1932

My dearest Ida!

Your last letter certifies that we both harbor the same thoughts. Since I had received your first letter, I really don't know what is going on with me. It has aroused a strong desire to receive frequent letters from you.

Perhaps the Christians are right in their judgment of the Jews. They say that the latter are very sensitive and intense. It is a fact that those of German descent are less impulsive and intense than we Jews.

I believe your Christian college friends don't beat their Jewish colleagues or lady friends either. The anti-Semitic storm here has passed and it is quite still now.

Now write often and much and I will follow your example.

Your Wolf

Wilno, Feb. 21, 1933

My dearest Ida:

Often a strong longing for you takes possession of me. How I can't wait to have you in my arms and shower your loving face with kisses.

I have learned all the ways to obtain a visa. The Hebrew Aid Society has helped me. My intentions are to come with an excursion to the Chicago Exposition. All necessary papers for this purpose are in full action. I am sure the consul will give me a tourist visa. I shall need a foreign visa, which must cost about $100. I hope to be at the consul about the first days of April. Excuse me for causing you certain expenses for the affidavit. I thought I'd try another way, the quota system. But as the quotas are in the hands of untrustworthy people who at their whim call this quota system law, it is very uncertain.

I can inform you about my own person. I am working very hard as an accountant in the Chopin Brewery. Some workers were laid off, but the work has increased and the wages decreased for the times are very hard here.

Yours with my best love, W

May 7, later in the day, 2000

Dear Dad,

I know you had trouble getting into the United States. Our once-liberal immigration laws, which welcomed Mom's parents in 1902, changed after World War I, so many fewer prevailed and managed to enter. You must have been so very determined. I am glad.

Love, Helaine

After 1918, prospective immigrants had to prove they had financial resources. In 1924, permanent quotas were set up and a visa and permit were required. This was partly to discourage the flood of Eastern Europeans trying to come to the United States.

Wilno, April 14, 1933

My dearest Ida:

It is spring now. The silvery moon spreads its light over the horizon. The night is splendid. All around is calm and charming. A patriarchal spirit seems to hover over the Jewish Vilna. I don't know how such a scene influences others, but it influences me greatly. After midnight, I roamed about the city in search of something I could not find. If you were here, I would surely have found it. But alas! In such evenings we could weave our fairy-tale while holding close to one another, or I could tell you some fables that we tell babies, and you would laugh heartily.

Nature, with her inexhaustible desire for life, impresses us with it, particularly in spring. Rightly does a Polish author express this feeling by calling it, "awakening spring." When this desire to hold you will be fulfilled is very hard to tell, but I believe that it will be. Meanwhile we must satisfy our desire with dreams trying to bring it to reality.

Last week I saw a movie which you would have liked. It is one about war titled "The Man Whom I Killed." It represents a battlefield on which a French soldier kills a German. The French soldier ransacks the dead soldier's pockets and finds some pictures of him and his bride on which some words of love are inscribed. His conscience pricks him for destroying a young life, and he decides to atone for his sin. He begins to bring flowers from time to time and lays them on the soldier's grave. There he meets the fallen soldier's bride who also brings flowers to decorate her lover's grave. He begins to follow her steps till they lead him to the dead man's parents' house with whom she lives. His father is a German physician. He frequents their house and they become quite devoted to him, including the bride. He often plays the dead man's violin; the same deep melodies that the other did. The parents' terrible longing for their lost son is calmed seeing a semblance of the dead in the living. The old joy has reawakened in their home. The parents propose to him to marry their son's bride and thus remain with them forever. This lures him on to confess his sin to them. Finally, they forgive him and adopt him. This picture was very attractive and emotional.

My best love, Wolf

Wilno, April 28, 1933

My Dearest Ida:

Summer is striding with large steps. Soon midsummer will come and we are still separated by distance. Not only are my thoughts taken up with this, but I am trying by all means available to get a visa. As far as my coming to the states as a tourist, all my papers are ready. Anyhow, I shall know everything on the fifth of May and shall let you know about it in a detailed letter.

People are upset here because of the inflation. The dollar has fallen. It has lost its value from ten to fifteen percent. Can you tell us what this means? Your Roosevelt is monopolizing the dollar and here it is losing its value. Our zlote can become worthier than your dollar if things go on in the same manner.

Are you having financial shocks now?

I remain with love

Wolf

Wilno, April 30, 1933

My dearest Ida,

After struggling six months with the consulate, I have regained all hope and desire to live and be with you in the nearest future. With what great impatience I am waiting for the day that shall unite us and we shall know the thrill of love which nature has granted us. Our motto shall be one of harmony and happiness.

Since I now have the visa in my pocket, every minute I am separated from you is like an eternity. Certain affairs that I must settle before starting keep me back. I am awaiting the journey plan, which the ship company has to send me. I shall choose a ship as soon as possible and let you know immediately.

Meanwhile, best love and regards to all and many kisses to you.

Wolf

Still May 7, 2000

Dad,

You surely sound like a young man in love. You also sound desperate to leave Europe. On one envelope, I found a note saying Mom realized she was deciding her future that will save your life. This note was certainly prophetic.

Love, Helaine

Wilno, May 17, 1933

My dearest Ida,

Returning from Warsaw on visa business, I found your long letter waiting for me. I am sure that all obstacles will be cast aside. I always have in mind that I only want to see you happy and content, certainly together with me.

Almost four years have passed since we have seen one another. My feelings for you have not changed. On the contrary, they have become stronger and more passionate. I am driven to you believing in a happy and prosperous future.

If it were only possible to come to you even as the blind passenger on the deck of the ship, I would gladly do so, but you know that America has created all difficulties for us Europeans, whereas Europe has made none for you Americans. That's a great injustice for us, but till this wrong can be improved, many tens of years can pass. But for me personally, with united strength, we can now improve this wrong.

I have written your parents a long detailed letter and have treated our problem of reuniting in its entirety.

With best wishes and love to you and all.

I remain forever,

Wolf

In Germany in 1933, Jewish persecution became Nazi policy under Chancellor Hitler.

Wilno, August 28, 1933

Dear and beloved friends Frank and Mary (Mom's parents) and family,

Your loving letter I did receive. It made me very happy to receive your letter, because I see in it the true fatherly devotion for which you are owed true thanks. Also, it makes me very happy that your economic situation has improved, and let me wish you that continued good fortune.

What are important are the immigration questions that I always have. Seeking the quest to travel and in order to give you some factual material, I have worked out various papers, but sorrowfully I am not yet able to get a permanent visa from the American Consul. I gave up the idea of a tourist one.

I am sending you a letter addressed to me from the Hebrew Immigrant Aid Society. So it seems now, that the Roosevelt Administration is getting a great deal more liberal than in the past. If there is hope for receiving the visa, we will certainly not have any difficulty. Please give to Ida a loving and heartfelt regard and the same to all of you.

Affectionately devoted, Wolf

Warsaw, Poland October 14, 1933

Consulate of the United States
To Wolf Shoag,

The General American Consulate cannot give you a tourist visa to the United States because our research shows that you are not eligible for tourist category article III 2nd in the Emigration Law. The General American Consulate found that the documents that you sent were examined carefully, but the information in these documents does not agree with the information regarding your property. Given this situation, the consulate will not change their decision about granting you a tourist visa.

Wilno, October 21, 1933

To the Consulate of the United States
Dear Consul:

As I wrote to you previously, I was in Warsaw at the office of the American Consul the 17th of October and handed in all the papers you sent me. I attached my own which should have served as a proof that I am well to do and a guarantee that I'll return to Poland after visiting my relations.

After cross-examining me, they told me to hand in another paper and then I'll receive the tourist visa. They hurried in sending me a refusal before I had time enough to deliver my papers to their office.

I can't understand such treatment and am at loss what to do next. The refusal is signed by Vice Consul Francis B. Stevens. The Number of my case 8II-II Shoag, Wolf.

Yours, Wolf Shoag

October 30, 1933

Dear Consul:

According to the consulate decision, based on information regarding my property, I have the honor to let you know it is a mistake. Please check again and find what I say is true. I explain that at the same address my relative Uncle Benjamin Shoag and his wife live, owners of house 51A with a market store. He has a son Wulfa who is now owner of the house and market. But I, Wolf, son of Moses Mattathias and Fagel Rochel, am the owner of the business and property at 51B. The above circumstances are confusing. This letter is to let you know that the information the consulate based its decision on is not about me, but about Wulfa, son of Benjamin and Devorah. I cordially ask you to look again. I'm expecting the consulate will try to find the true answer and will clear the situation.

With respect,

Wolf Shoag

March 5, 1934

The consulate of the United States
To Wolf Shoag,

The General American Consulate announces that you can come to this office any day you like to be re-interviewed about your petition for a tourist visa. Bring with you a valid passport to travel to the United States and return to Poland.

March 8, 1934

My dearest Ida,

The fifth year is passing since we came to know one another. Our acquaintance was a short one but a thoroughly hearty one. Many waters have flowed on since, but they were unable to abandon my warm feelings to you.

Darling Ida! When you left here I felt as if I were walking in a dream. I couldn't find any rest. Your generosity and your clever, penetrating eyes filled me with a feeling of adoration. Your whole being with its high intelligence had pierced into my very soul. Even then in my dreams I took possession of you, but I didn't understand it. After your departure, I plunged into the studying of a strange language with the whole passion of knowledge that was to give me the possibility of understanding you and making myself understood. This took two years and I wrote and waited with patience. I couldn't understand your thoughts, as your life's routine was strange to me. Perhaps you loved another man then? And that was why I interrupted my correspondence, still feeling deep respect to your person.

Not one proposal was made to another after I met you, and I had met quite suitable girls, but none equal to you.

One autumn day the sun suddenly spread its caressing bright rays over the whole horizon. Your first letter, after a long pause, came and added to the pleasure felt on such a day. This was in October 1932. Your letter dictated serious desires and again my thoughts were carried to you over the ocean. Your letters were full of hope as were mine, but the distance seemed to frighten you. Sometimes you seemed to despair until your father sent me the papers.

A blooming period began for me. My joy, that our meeting was so near, was indescribable. Your letters then stated the same.

With great energy I took to destroy distance and never thought that I wouldn't conquer it. Whether one way or another, measures have been taken. The thing is done. I am called to get the visa.

Thanks for the papers and I would thank you for more if possible.

Your ever-loving, Wolf

May 21, 1934
A letter from Ida said "Please Hurry."

May 29, 1934

To Wolf Shoag

You are booked on the United States Lines the ship "Manhattan" leaving from Havre on June 7th, 3rd class cabin cost $107.

THE MID 1930s

In 1935, Germany passed the Nuremberg Racial Laws disenfranchising those of Jewish blood. Jewish businesses were boycotted or stolen. Anti-Semitism spread rapidly as German policy influenced the Poles and Lithuanians. Frightened Jews looked to the Soviet Union for protection when a Vilna synagogue was set on fire in 1935. By 1937, Polish universities were discriminating against Jewish students. German and Eastern European leaders tried to deprive Jews of their spiritual leaders as well.

May 8, 2000

Dear Dad,

Difficult as it was for you, you were among the lucky to obtain papers to emigrate. By 1934 you were in Jeannette, PA married to Mom and managing the rug department in Grandpa Frank Levin's Furniture Store. Soon you had two children. You were safe and busy trying to get your family out of Europe. Trying to sell shoes and dry goods from their house, they were becoming destitute; a reason why the Jews looked to Russia.

I found this letter dated March 1938 from United States Congressman Robert Allen from Greensburg, PA to the American Consul in Warsaw asking him to help get Aunt Sonia's husband, Rabbi David Cypkiewitz, out. You had managed to get him a job offer at the Chevra Shalom Synagogue in Jeannette. He was to come with his family. But even a congressman's influence didn't help with the

American Consulate in Warsaw, and, tragically, the effort failed. You must have felt so guilty. I'm sorry for your pain. I know you tried. They knew you tried.

It is late and getting dark. I am going back to our wonderful French hotel to have dinner in the café next door with my group. Dinner is always a baked potato filled with meat and mushrooms, but I love it. I'm home with my ancestors.

Helaine

THE LATE 1930s

May 10, 2000

Dear Dad,

We were driven to Kaunas, Kovno to you in Yiddish, still the second largest city in Lithuania. Were you ever there? There is a lovely Eighteenth Century walking promenade with stores on either side of a tree-lined median. Not far away, the Japanese consulate building has a sign dedicating the building to Chiune Sugihara who bravely gave visas to Jews, allowing them to escape in the early 1940s, even though his government prohibited it. Those who could escape went through Japan to Shanghai, China.

Did you ever see the Nineteenth Century Fort Nine Prison built by a Russian Tsar right outside of the city? In 1941, it was used as a place to imprison and then shoot Jews, including those from Germany and France. Thirty thousand were killed. We were taken to see the small cells where prisoners were kept. As expected, they were dark and dank. In the field next to the prison stands a huge, powerful monument to commemorate the dead. The monument is carved in light-brown stone and looks like tortured people. Stone arms are uplifted and stone faces cried out. I'll never get the picture out of my mind.

H

Monument at Fort Nine Prison

By 1939, even before the German invasion of Poland, war conditions prevailed. Jews fled eastward. Vilna became overcrowded. There was a shortage of fuel and food. Mail was censored and erratic. Radios were confiscated.

Vilna, May 11, 2000

Dear Dad,

It is a bright new day and I'm back at your old house. How lucky I am that I am here. I came back to this bench near your old home to read the letters Grandpa Moses and Aunt Roza wrote to you in 1939 before the Vilna Ghetto was formed in 1941. I am trying to understand this family that I never knew.

Grandpa Moses and Aunt Roza, with her flowery Yiddish, were trying to remain hopeful. These letters are so painful. I've been crying all day. If I could write to them, I'd tell them how I long to know them and feel desperate for their suffering. I now understand how unbelievably terrible it was for you knowing what you did, trying to help and not being able to.

Having seen some mementos to terror for myself, I've taken my head out of the sand. I read these letters from Moses and Roza with new understanding of your speechlessness. This was not only your problem. It was a problem of humanity. I read these letters and weep.

Vilna, August 28, 1939

Dear Son,

May you live, with your good wife Ida and raise your children to long and good years. Amen

Today I am not a bearer of good news. Today there was a mobilization. Today they summoned all the young men. It is a sure death. God knows what will happen. We are greatly in debt because we spent half the winter being ill. Then in summertime we sent money to your brother Israel in Myadel, Belarus, who is ill with TB. These bad times tear at bones and skin and God knows when I will receive support from you. We don't know what to do. Maybe it is possible for you to send us money. Have a healthy year.

We are starting to say farewell. Our hooligans are sharpening their wolfish teeth. May they not live to accomplish their plans. We do not know whether to stay or leave! You must understand. Pour on the help. It is right to do so because we cannot get to the Promised Land, Israel. England must mobilize the world! The world acts as if it knows nothing, sees nothing!

Moses

On the same letter is a note from Aunt Roza.

Sonia and Roza Shoag

O my child, I am not a happy mother. Weep! Beg God about this Destruction.

Dear and most beloved children, from the bottom of my heart, I send love to the big children and to our dearest little children.

The long, good years have now flown away. The wives and the children and parents and all the limbs are torn away. Today all is lost. We try not to let ourselves die from hunger. Destiny has fallen upon you that you should feed us.

We must make a decision whether to move to Traube. One might be safer in the little towns than the city. Maybe we will be able to go there to save ourselves from death.

Your ever-loving sister Roza

May 12, 2000

Dear Dad,

I cannot believe this next sad letter. It was written two days before the War started! They knew what was going to happen to them. They must have known. How awful. Dad, I see Grandpa and Roza both wrote this letter so it must have been written in this very house.

Love, Helaine

Monday the 12th day of Elul 8/28, 1939
(Page 1 from Moses)

Dear children of ours, Frank, Mary, (Levin, Ida's parents) and our dear children Wolf, Ida, our beloved sweet grandchildren,

We can already say goodbye. God knows if we will be able to recognize one another. We have already had the taste of war for four and a half years in 1914–1918. The war could then have made us crazy from the sorrow. We were left here crippled. The blood running through us could have turned to pus. This did not happen. We were then young and strong. Today the streets are full of bloody cries. The women run after the men, the children after the fathers. One cries hysterically. No one can take any more. Hunger chases us. The horses were taken away even from the Gentiles. There is one horse left in a whole village.

We Jews cannot bring anything into the city. One is without teeth. Who has the strength or means to fight the enemy? Ah, Wolf! How can you listen to this? How our enemies want to make nothing from Jewish possessions. How hard everything was accumulated. One can write nothing in these letters. One comforts oneself believing that America will come to our defense. It should not be, God forbid, how it was for the Jews when the Destruction of Jerusalem took place. Others promised to help but did not. Scream with all your might that one should really save a people from destruction. One pinches oneself all the while and one tears chunks of flesh and blood runs readily. And people still play politics.

My heart is broken over my load of poverty. Where shall we put ourselves? Everyone wants to eat. I must scream over the seas to all my friends. No one must hold back help in such a time. During the first war, a fire broke out from God. I remember the panic—how people used to lie in the streets, swollen from hunger. How we used to get a little flour from some of the Germans who understood our speech as old German. They were here for four and a half years. I used to share with everyone. I used to say, "Children, such a time to do good and to share with the poor." God answered us that our family did not die from hunger.

All our dear ones, are we not, God forbid, parting forever? Forgive me that I cry with all my might. It is that it hurts so much from that other war. Who can feel our pain as well as you, my child? There was no bread. And some of us were ruined after that war and became beggars until we were put in the grave. Today is a worse danger than the other war. I was still so heroic then even though we had over us the Cossacks, the Bolshevists. One overcame the time and remained alive. For you and Roza my eyes did not dry four years. When the war first started, I should not have sent you with the store goods to Orsha, Belarus when you were only ten years old and Roza was only fourteen. We were cut off for four long years, you in Orsha and we in Vilna, but you came home. And now, cry again. Cry not to know where some of my children are. That is to me worse than everything. Our life is so bad now, what do we have to save?

(On the same letter Roza writes)

My dear ones and most beloved ones, from the bottom of my heart I pray you should be healthy and strong, happy and lucky. You should not know from any war.

We received your letter, my child, written on the evening before Yom Kipper. We thank you for your wanting to know about us. We were left living, thank God. We answered you right away on a postcard. We also sent a long letter; whether it came to you or not, we do not know. For the time is naturally not a quiet one. We did not receive the $20 that you sent at the holiday time. If you can, ask for it back.

We live as poorly as Hitler should live. We might still attain something good in our older years. If you will be able to write us, write us. Do not hold back. So is it that one struggles in life for nothing. Left lonely, separated from the most loved of our heart. We thank God we are alive during this second war.

My son Shlomo is already registered as an electrical technician. He may enlist in the Russian army. Who can stand this much sadness. Oh, my sick heart!

You have already had a blessed year with your son Aryah's birth. We are blessed…certainly. I kiss myself with all of you. I press you strongly to my heart. I had hoped that we would yet some time see one another. Our hopes did not come true. On the hills, the military is encamped with all their ammunition. It can be that they will, God forbid, tell us to go away from here. Perhaps I am writing too much. But no one is alone. This letter writes itself: it cries itself. No one wants to be killed. Like this at least we will die with honor. God knows where one will be thrown.

One wants at least to have letters from you. This is dearer than my life. God knows if we will hear anything from our children. If it is possible for you to send anything to us, you should send only to our address.

Your ever-loving sister, Roza

On September 1, 1939, Germany invaded Poland and World War II began. The Red army conquered Belarus and Ukraine on September 17, 1939. On October 10, 1939, the USSR took Vilna back from Poland and returned it to Lithuania. Polish Jews fled there and anti-Jewish riots broke out in the city from October 28 to 31.

Post card October 31, 1939 from M. Shoag and Roza, Wilno, Wilcomieska 51

Sonia's bridegroom Rabbi Ciepkievitz walked 3 weeks by foot from Warsaw to Myadel, Belarus to find out if brother Israel and his family were alive. When we will be able, we'll write about what happened here. My dear children, it truly has become a Destruction. Thank God we are alive. Children ours, may you be healthy and strong. Write soon about the dear, loving, little ones.

Roza

In November the Jews began to organize their own defenses.

November 1, 1939

Beloved dear Wolf, little wife Ida, and family,

We have lived through this terror to see a letter from you. We have, God be thanked, all gone through the seven roads of Hell, but Hell is not finished yet. The planes have flown over us, flown by the crooked hands of the enemy. In 1940, we will have to get 350,000 Jews out from the midst of all the dangers from the war. People have no rest and the war has just begun. If it were not for the Red Army, we would, God Forbid, already be "guests among the dead."

We are just now, thank God, under the sovereignty of Lithuania. In five days things will be in order. Now the prices are high. Bread costs one silver zlotes per kilo. Food is in short supply and is dear. The $20 that you sent us last time we did not receive. Did you get it back? We beg you; send us as much money as possible. The letters went through Moscow to Kaunas and, since Vilna has become Lithuania, we finally received a letter through Kaunas.

Wolf, our siblings Israel, Sonia, and Beyle are alive, but the flaw is that only God knows when we will see them.

We greet our loved, dear in-laws from the heart. Frank and Mary, may they live long. We wish them happiness from all their children.

Roza

Moses continues this letter.

Most beloved, dearest everyone,

From the bottom of our hearts be well. I wish all the children, especially your dear little ones, health and strength. May your times be better than ours.

Thank God we all remain alive. The grandchildren have fled to Russia. Conditions here in Vilna are no good. Roza wanted to write a lengthy letter about it. God knows if I will live to receive another letter. With a word, we stay alive. If we live, there will be something to tell. Vilna was lucky that the Red Army came right away. If not, it would have been a blood bath for the Jews. Jews in other parts of Lithuania have, poor dears, been slaughtered like cows. From time to time, Germans will still drag Jews through the streets. Vilna has remained because of a miracle. She is blessed and she should of course be blessed.

We go without bread. One needs to dig with their hands for their potatoes, for there are none to buy and no money. In about two months, thank God, even this will change and spring may bring some new potatoes to our little plot. We take every bite to our mouths with willingness remembering the memory of the taste. The thought in my bones is the pained knowledge that more may not come.

The SS must know what has happened to some of our people. What is happening in America?

Moses

November 3, 1939

My dear brother,

My dear children, what a world! Days go by that we do not receive a bite of bread or potato. Bread costs five zlotes. Whoever has anything to trade can do so because the Christians want money. What you sent did not arrive, but the package did come from Nathan. Why is it that God in Heaven made Jews and then has them and their good deeds destroyed? The peasants do not go to market as they are frightened. We do not have money to buy anything from the Russians. Today, my children, you can already believe the memory of having been satisfied with food is gone.

And when children fly away, parents' hearts are broken. It would be good to see each other. But sadly, only God knows when. Let it be enough for today. I am alive. Our sister Beyle and her husband already left here long ago for Minsk. We have letters from them to us.

Do NOT send any food packages. They will be stolen.

Roza

Vilna, Nov. 5, 1939

My loved and dearest ones, from the bottom of my heart, brother and sister and dear children, healthy, strong and happy may you all be.

It is hard never to see and hear from you. What we all have lived through and seen and heard is impossible to describe. What we have seen in seven and a half weeks is generally impossible to write except in books. But thank God, we have all remained alive. Now like sheep, we will have to teach ourselves Lithuanian! This language is very foreign to us and unintelligible. Wolf, my child, your letter brought much joy and we simply wept for joy because you still care for us and still worry about us in such a bitter time, even from afar. Let me remind you of all good things that happened in the past. I want so much to talk things over with you, my dearest one, and tell you every thing, everything. But it is impossible here. Everyone is paralyzed and cannot speak. If God will have mercy on us and we will survive to see a future, we will have had in truth been visited by the Messiah. But for this short time, we have seen nothing from God. We still hope for peace and I have taken care of our sick, lonely parents. Everyone is separated from us. God knows for how long. All the grandchildren came to say farewell to all of us and to buy something. Of course, buying is fraught with difficulties. Well, as long as we are alive we have seen such interesting periods in history. In my life I would never have dreamed about what we have had in reality. I hope that we will be able to remain in written contact with everyone but God knows if our letter will get through. Whatever you read about us believe it all. It will not be exaggerated!

You understand that one must live. From afar I press you all to my heart and kiss you from afar. Greetings to your in laws and wish them much good. I beg a favor. If by chance you write to our brother Shia in Israel, from whom I received $10 for which I have not thanked him. Thank him for me. I bought a little bit of wood with it. God forbid, if I had not had that bit of wood we would have been lost. May God hold him in Peace in this world.

Roza

Vilna, November 30, 1939

Dear Wolf,

The Lithuanians under the Russians have renamed our street Filima Gotva. They have renamed practically all of the streets.

Betty, Aunt Leah's daughter got married to an electrician. Her husband is very handsome and a very decent man. The Bolsheviks have moved the entire factory and the workers back to Russia so Betty and her husband are now in Russia. Her husband has left the factory and gone to the conservatory to study voice. Soon he is scheduled to perform on the radio. Cousin Fanya has also gotten married to a good friend of hers. So our dear relations in the house in front, Uncle Benjamin and Aunt Devorah, now just take care of the great-grandmother.

For today let it be enough to write. I beg you, my child, don't lose touch with me. You are my only written communication. So I have hoped that we will all see one another in good health. We must meanwhile forget about such pleasure. Be you, my brother, healthy and strong and happy, with your wife and dear children.

My husband and children greet you heartily and wish you all that is good.

If it is not difficult for you to send the bit of money, I would be glad. Try to send a few dollars for I owe 600 zlotes. There is a very huge contrast in the price. The banks take out 16 percent to 18 percent.

Your not forgotten sister, Roza Koslovska

POSTAL TELEGRAM 10/ 27 Mother died. Received the money.

Vilna, December 6, 1939

My dearest ones,

From the bottom of my heart, brother, sister and dearest children, may you always be healthy, strong and happy.

Having received your long awaited letter today, my brother, I hurry to answer you. This is a letter you sent out 9.10 .39. It has taken three months to reach us.

You ask, my brother, how you can send a little support, which is urgently needed. Money letters go to Kaunas via telegraph. Life already is a little more normal here. Those who have now been able to survive this bitter and unfortunate time will be able to go on living.

Father is seriously ill. He has severe asthma. It unfortunately doesn't let him lie down or sleep. I am just about to take him to the hospital. May God have pity already upon me and let him survive so that I may be able to bring him home.

I have become very lonely. The children have all remained in Russia. Full goblets of troubles have been placed before me. Of course this is my heavy misfortune, one cannot run away anywhere, kid. That's the way it is, kid.

For today it is enough to write. In a later letter I will write you more, my brother.

My husband and my children greet you very affectionately.

Roza Koslovska

Vilna, December 20, 1939

My dear ones,

I send you greetings and love from the bottom of my heart, brother and sister and dear children. Just be healthy and strong.

My dearest brother, I am not at all clear about the time since I have heard from anyone. I simply don't know any longer what to think. Everyone has received letters and we—nothing. Not from you, not from Shia and not from our other brothers and sisters. Look, kid, don't be stingy, write a few words. Perhaps you can contact Shia and tell him Uncle Benjamin is not well. He was in the hospital. If possible, if everyone could send something, it would be very welcome.

Be comforted, kissed. I press you to my heart. I want an answer and then I will write you a long letter.

Roza

Vilnius, December 26, 1939

RE: cable 220=$30
To American Savings
Honored H. Brown

We received the money in the sum of $177.60 from Wolf Shoag in America through your banking house. We thank you very much.

Yours, Moses Shoag

P.S. I ask you to forward my letter to Mr. Shoag in America. This is very important and necessary.

Vilna Dec. 26, 1939

My most beloved ones, from my whole heart, brother and sister and darling children, be only healthy, strong and happy.

I am answering you promptly, brother, upon the receipt of the tele-gram and money, which father, may he be well, has received. However much it was, it was very useful. Father lay in the Jewish hospital across the street. Do you perhaps remember it? Then he began to feel better, so I took him to my house for a while. On Fri-day, he was able to travel to the post with my son Shlomo to pick up the money.

Then he began to feel sick and got a high fever, so high that he needed a doctor right away. We had to bring him back to the hos-pital and he is still there. His condition is grave and serious. What can we, my child, do to help? If tears were a good remedy he would surely get well quickly. Because mainly, from everything and everybody, my eyes are never dry.

I have remained very lonely. The children have all remained in Rus-sia.

From Sonia, I have great anguish. The news from her is not very good. They imprisoned her husband, the dear Rabbi that you tried to bring to the United States. God knows what they will do with him. I hear from them seldom. One cannot speak together, nor cor-respond as before, but that's the way it is, my child. You can't go against the times. When the time comes, she takes her due. In the whole world one cannot find a hero that can go against the times. The time is mightier and stronger than anyone, even if you are healthy.

From Beyle, I had a greeting, but from Israel nothing. We wanted to bring Israel here from Belarus with his family but it is very costly and very difficult. Naturally, with a border it is no small thing.

We might be able to bring Sonia and her family, because there is hunger and poverty especially for religious people, but it is not possible for the moment. Maybe God will permit it, or maybe I will be able to help, via some of our friends. Everything is the same. We have come through the stormy times, thank God. What God wishes to give further, no one knows at all. One waits. It is not the end yet.

May you and your family be healthy, strong and happy. Your ever remembering, happiness wishing sister, Roza Koslovska.

Write me if letters go from America to Russia? If I get an answer from you promptly, I will write a big letter.

January 9, 1940 POSTAL TELEGRAPH Father died. It takes a long time to write. Send money.

More written on May 12, 2000
Oh, my goodness, Dad! Poor Aunt Roza. What a burdened but capable woman she was. I wish I had met her. H

Vilna, January 10, 1940

My dearest ones, from my heart brother and sister and beloved little children, only healthy, strong and happy should you always be.

The fifth time that I shall, my dear brother, write this letter. The pen falls from my hand and my heart and hands tremble as I write. I have to be the only one to tell not such good news. But, my child, I am the only fortunate, happy child of our "sainted parents" who was present from the very first moment mother became ill till the moment when they breathed out their holy souls. Our dear little mother, that holy soul, became ill Friday evening and was saved until Sunday early morning, around 4A.M. No doctors, apothecaries, nurses, tears were lacking. But nothing helped her. The contract came to a close. Now listen my child what our holy Mother told me ten minutes before her death. I was standing near her bed and the tears were pouring out without my will. She raised her head and says, " Listen my child, I too had a mother. I beg that you should be a mensch, (a mature person) not to cry and not to scream. A mother doesn't live forever. My few years were a gift. More I did not ask from God. Let me die in Peace." She laid her hands upon my head and blessed me. With clever understanding, with the beautiful loving expression, she quietly left me bereft and alone beside her bed.

And father, of blessed memory, is no longer here. I cannot yet write of them, may they rest in Peace. May they be good intercessors for their children that they should obtain all good things for us. They were, in these times, holy ones and the funeral orations were exceptional. Of course, the people accorded them much great honor, as the truly righteous and interred them both, hand by hand. Our dear mother died 3 Kislev, Nov. 26, 1939, our father five days in Tevat, Dec. 29, 1939.

Father survived the thirty-day mourning period plus two days after mother. When I returned from the cemetery and went to visit father in the hospital, he answered me that Mother is lucky and that he envied her. That is how the world is, my child. There is nothing to do. Maybe it really was a gift that they should die.

Let it be given, my child, that we should live as long as they did with such heart and honor and a good name. I have not yet written to any of the other children as freely as you, my child. I can't make myself do it yet. I just beg of God and our holy parents that this terrible news should do no harm to anyone. That is my prayer to God. But they must know because they must say the Kaddish pray for the dead. I'm afraid to write anything to Israel because he was very ill this summer. Maybe he will recover.

From now on write me a few words. You know, my child, today it will be my only comfort. From the children I hear nothing at all. Maybe if I can calm down, I will hear something from someone on the street. I will have greetings also. The sympathy comes from all corners.

I have not yet received the $25, because I am not at my address. I have remained deeply in debt; that you certainly understand, my child. Who knows when I will also be able to pay for the funerals. I wanted them to be as good and beautiful as possible, so that no one could say they died poor and alone. On the contrary, everyone wondered that I alone was able to do all this. I managed with fine embossed siddurs (prayer books) and everything. May they plead for us, for you and me, and for all their relations and good friends, may nothing hinder them, God forbid. Let it be enough for today. I hope yet to write to another sibling. I beg you, my child, take it all quietly, passively, with equanimity. I have wept enough for us all. Be healthy, strong and happy. Observe their Kaddish.

And let there be much, much good for you. I will again go to the cemetery and I will again ask of them much good for all us children. Be strong and happy.

Your happiness-wishing sister Roza Kozlovska

Also do not forget to write. Write about your children. How are your business affairs? In general how goes it?

Again May 12, 2000

Dear Dad,

These letters are astounding. I am at the death scene of a woman I look just like, whom I never knew. I have her round face and features and we are both a bit overweight. You loved her and described her as wonderfully kind and smart. She ran the store, while Moses went to synagogue. She was very charitable to the poor. It is remarkable that family myths are taken so seriously. I have gone to graduate school and become a social worker. Was it in my mind to be like her? It is my amazing luck to feel that I am at her deathbed. How wise she was. I will tell my own daughter the same truth about mothers dying.

Imagine dealing with not only war but also with sick and then dead parents. Aunt Roza was an amazing woman. I finally know her by reading these letters sixty-one years later. It has been my supreme privilege to be with Roza and Grandmother in her death scene. What marvelous women! I see why you loved them.

How prophetic Roza said it was a gift that your parents should die. They didn't have to experience what was coming. Moses seemed to know.

I am overwhelmed by my feelings! What must it have been for you, I can not imagine.

Helaine

Vilna, January 23, 1940

My loved ones, from the bottom of my heart, brother, sister, and dear little children. May you only be healthy, strong and happy.

Two weeks ago, Uncle Benjamin's daughter Mashal, brought me a second letter of yours. She brought me also a letter of yours from Shia in which there lay a check for $10, which I must send you back because it is in father's name. Reading over your letter, my child, gave my heart a little courage. But your last letter, my brother, is full of sorrow and tears. Of course, losing such holy, good, pious parents almost in one month is a great outcry in heaven, and being without the children nearby, the pain is even worse.

But what, my child, will now help us? If God wills it, it will happen. Their contracts have ended. It seems to you, that it is, God forbid, your fault, because of material help. No brother, you should quickly get that out of your mind. You should not think that I spared any money. You may believe me that money flowed like water. I overlooked nothing. Father lacked no medical help. They only lacked more years. Our parents, may they rest in peace, used to say, "Little children, if God forbid, there is an illness one must first be silent, but if there is a danger one must go out in the streets and scream Horror! I, from the first second, screamed Horror! But nothing helped any longer. Our dear father, may he rest in peace, contracted a strong asthma. The doctor confided to him a secret that he was even sicker than mother and he could not guarantee that he would live. Yet still he survived another thirty-two days.

After dear Mother's death I was with him in the house and watched him like the eyes of my head. Then I took him to the hospital where he lay for ten days. He got a little better and the doctors sent him home. So I took him to my house. You understand that no appropriate remedies were lacking for him. I wish he would have been less sad, but obviously he missed his good, pure, faithful wife every step of the way. He paid out to Uncle Benjamin the first $35 that you sent with his own hands. Maybe the hard, bitter winter hurt them. But whatever the reason, the fact remains that they are not here. It hurts me more than anyone, maybe because I witnessed it all with my own eyes and my own hands. Both died. Alone I led them to their Eternal Rest. I bought them beautiful resting places. Good rest and peace may it be unto them. And may they intercede for our children, our children's children, all our good friends and us all. By today's standards, they were holy, good, pious people. Of course we raised the money to pay the debts which I incurred on their behalf. Everyone gave me whatever I needed. Now they ask for it back. I can delay payment for a short time. I even arranged a monthly Kaddish for Mother Dear and a second Kaddish for Father Dear. I have not written my children this news because my heart did not let me. I also have not written our siblings, not Israel, Shia or Beyle or Sonia. It is difficult for me to tell them all the bad news at one time.

Therefore I write you thus: we could say that they lived out their years, as the Rabbis have said in their books. They did not leave any young children, God Forbid. They sent out into the world nice, fine and honest children. But it is still a loss that such people go away from the world. They were a model to the world of piety, goodness and honesty. May we all have such long, good years. Father was seventy-four and Mother sixty-nine. I beg you, my child, comfort yourself. Be a good father to your beautiful, good, little children. Also, understandably, we must weep very hard. One must know how to weep for an old mother and father. I had enough friends to help me weep, BUT THE WOUND IS MINE AND OURS.

Now, my child, give me some advice about what I should do. I can correspond with you now more easily because the mail can go through Russia. For the moment, it takes six weeks to get mail. It is hard to correspond with our brother Israel in Belarus. Before her death, our dear Mother begged me to bring Israel and his family to the house, but it is impossible. It is bound up with great problems. Usually, it is possible, but what to do? Our parents' home should be torn down but it tears my heart; so much hard work went on there. On the Sabbath I am going to take a look at the broken house.

Uncle Benjamin is already unofficially 82 years, may he live long and happily. He is still clever. I worry about him in the current winter because the winter is a hard one with frost and blizzards. For the old ones, this winter is very difficult.

It is hard for me to decide to leave the city for Traube. Maybe I can borrow a little money in the store and make fancy goods from a little paper. But for that you need money. That's what's the matter, not how to take care of the houses but how to make a living. It is a great question. Mother, may she be blessed, would want it to stay up. For the moment, there are refugees in the house, Yeshiva students. The Yeshiva students study there all day. They have a great merit and worth. I await your advice about them. Alone, I don't want to do anything and I don't know what to do. I am as if waking up from a terrible nightmare.

The telegram to father with $25 I sent back along with the check of $10. However, they are very needed for the debts. If you can, please send them again in my name:

Kozlovska Roza Zawalna
34/6 Pylimo gatwe

Dear Dad,

The last word we have from Roza was sent to Uncle Shia in Palestine. It is ironic that she hopes that they shall all meet again. H

Postcard May 26, 1940
My dear and beloved brother Shia and sister and beloved children—be only healthy and strong and happy.

I came to an agreement with your father (in-law) Joseph (Kantorovieins) about the gift Wolf sent to me. We decided that you should keep it. I wish from the bottom of my heart that you should use it in the best of health with a happy heart. I await mail from the children, but so far nothing. We wait and we hope for better. Write what is going on with you. How do you live? You should only be healthy and live and we will know all good things. Unfortunately it is now difficult to tell all. If God will give us the possibility, we will again see each other and be together.

Be healthy and strong, your well-wishing sister, Roza Kozlovska.

May 13, 2000 back at the hotel

Dear Dad,

I was profoundly shaken re-reading these letters here, as you can tell. My wise guide Regina, who was with me, was "blown away" too. I asked her how feelings were running here now. Her answer was that, although things look good, the economy is going downhill after ten years of independence from the Communists. When the economy becomes bad, people look for others to blame. They look for scapegoats.

I asked because as we made our way slowly back to the hotel through the busy streets, I was heartbroken to see "Zuden Rout" (Jews out) graffiti on a street wall. The small, quaint-looking antique shop above had three identical new posters in the window. They showed a waist-up colored picture of Hitler in a khaki uniform with the words "Hitler Isvaduotojas" ("Hitler Savior" in Lithuanian). There were other new posters of Hitler in the back. Anti-Semitism never died here.

Love, Helaine

Hitler Savior

Jew out

Vilna, May 14, 2000

Dear Dad,

Tomorrow we leave for home. How can I tell you this and cause you so much heartache. We went to the Paneriai Forest, ten miles from Vilna. Paner is a place of contrast, peaceful woods where the Lithuanians and Nazis committed terrible atrocities. There is a large stone Genocide Memorial in the clearing with an inscription commemorating the 100,000 killed: 70,000 were Jews.

Five clearings had been dug for large oil pits to accommodate the trains that came through during the earlier part of the century. In 1941, people were lined around an oil pit and shot. They fell inward and were buried. We suspect that along with other Vilna citizens, Aunt Roza Shoag Koslovska was taken there. It breaks my heart to tell you this for I know she was closer to you than anyone. I'm sorry that you wanted to know.

I learned from the Internet that Uncle Israel and his family were killed in Myadel, Belarus in 1941. Sonia and her family were killed in the town in northern Lithuania where they were living. I don't know what happened to Aunt Beyle.

You cried for three days when you went to see your brother Uncle Shia in Israel. After forty years of feeling guilty for not bringing you here, how glad I am that you didn't return. No one is left. You would not have been able to bear the pain. It was ordained that I came in your place. Like Roza, I've cried for us all, for your family that I should have had the privilege to know. Words cannot tell you that I needed to bear witness for you—without you.

Love, Helaine

Historic References

Arad, Yitzhak. (1985) Ghetto in Flames: The Struggle and Destruction of the Jews in Vilna in the Holocaust. New York: Holocaust Library.

Davidowicz, Lucy S.(1986) The War Against the Jews 1933–1945. New York: Bantam Books.

Dimont, Max I. (1994) Jews, God and History. New York: Bantam Books.

Encyclopedia Britannica (1965). "Immigration Law." Vol. 11, pp. 1102–1105.

Greenbaum, Masha. (1995) The Jews of Lithuania: a History of a Remarkable Community 1316–1945. Jerusalem: Gefen.

Literary References

Cohen, Rich. (2000) The Avengers: A Jewish War Story. New York: Alfred Knopf.

Fremont, Helen. (1999) After Long Silence: A Memoir. New York: Delta Trade Paperback.

Oshry, Ephraim Rabbi. (1995) The Annihilation of Lithuanian Jewry. New York: The Judaica Press.

Polt, Renata. (1999) A Thousand Kisses: A Grandmother's Holocaust Letters. Tuscaloosa: The University of Alabama Press.

Siegal, Aranka (1994) Upon the Head of the Goat: A Childhood in Hungary 1939–1944. New York: Puffin Books.

978-0-595-39737-2
0-595-39737-9

Printed in the United States
51696LVS00002B/1-51